By His Mercy

How 11 Ordinary Young Catholics have seen
God's Extraordinary Mercy

By His Mercy

How 11 Ordinary Young Catholics have seen God's Extraordinary Mercy

Tricia Walz
Leah Wienhold
Sally Traut
Fr. Doug Liebsch
Amanda Vasek
Jessica Vasek
Nicole (Nikki) Walz
Fr. Derek Wiechmann
Hannah Molitor
Molly McGowan
Cathryn Senour

Foreward by Fr. Russell Kovash
Cover by Isabel Drake

Tricia Walz
2018

First Printing: 2018

ISBN: 978-1-387-50101-4

Tricia Walz
Saint Cloud, MN 56303

Cover Artist: Isabel Drake

Contents

Acknowledgements

We would like to thank all of the priests and religious brothers and sisters who have given their lives to the Lord. We are eternally grateful for all that you do! We would also like to thank our family and friends without whose help this book would never have been completed. Thank you for all the prayers and support!

Foreword

In 1 Corinthians 9:24-27, St. Paul likens the Christian life to running a race. And what do we know about races? Well, they can often be very challenging to complete. If we take a marathon, for example, (26.2 miles), all kinds of challenges can present themselves to the athletes running the race. There can be strong winds and heavy rains, a hot sun or cold temperatures, all of which can add to the difficulty of the race. Injuries, both new ones and the aggravation of old ones, can hamper one's running. Fatigue, coupled with the things already mentioned, can prompt the runner to quit the race or considering quitting, or at least have doubts about actually being able to finish it. As I read the stories of these eleven young Catholics, it confirmed in me just how difficult the "race" of the Christian life can be for us. Despite all the joys, blessings, and good times in life, all of us are deeply aware that our lives are often filled with immense challenges, confusion, pain and suffering, profound loss, sadness, and heartbreak. While Jesus exclaimed that He came to our earth so that we would have life and have it more abundantly, He was also brutally honest with us in letting us know that down here below, in our imperfect world, we would have troubles and that each of us would have to carry our cross. But He also assured us that we are to have courage for He has overcome the world.

The stories you are about to read involve many of the challenges we human beings face as we run the race of faith on this earth. You will hear about life-threatening illnesses, the tragic loss of loved ones, uncertainty about God's will in one's life, personal struggles and weaknesses, brushes with death, and doubts about God's existence and the mystery of His ways. But amidst these challenges, you will also hear of extraordinary physical and spiritual healings, the granting of supernatural peace, acceptance, and guidance during times of doubt, confusion, and loss, the incredible providence of God, and the outrageous love and mercy He has for us, his prized creation.

As I read and re-read these stories, two things kept coming back to my heart. First, all things are possible with God. And second, God never abandons us in our trials, tribulations, and struggles. We are not in this race alone. God is always present and is always working in our lives, although often in ways we did not expect or could not comprehend. Both of these truths ought to fill us with great hope amidst the uncertainties of life. Christian hope is flat-out necessary for us in life. It allows us, not to bypass the darkness and trials and tribulations of life, but to pass through them, on our way to our final end. Hope lifts our eyes above the things here below which disappoint us and often sock us in the gut, taking our breath away. Hope tells us that this life does not have the final say. It inspires us to keep getting up in the morning, to keep walking, struggling, searching, praying, and loving.

In the book *Beautiful Hope* put out by Dynamic Catholic, there appears a thought-provoking quote from an unknown author about the necessity of hope. It says this: "Man can live forty days without food, about three days without water, about eight minutes without air, but only one-second without hope." Oh how true it is that we need hope!! May these stories inspire us to keep running the race of faith and may they increase our supernatural hope, the hope that not only is God always with us amidst our trials and tribulations, but that His love and mercy will bring each of us safely home to heaven.

Fr. Russell Kovash
October 2018

Tricia Walz

"We can never have too much hope in God.
He gives in the measure we ask."

-St. Thérèse of Lisieux

God bless you!!
♡Tricia Walz

"Miracle: An extraordinary event manifesting
divine intervention in human affairs"
– Merriam Webster Dictionary

It was that time of year: the time when most kids start dreading the day the flu shot becomes available everywhere you go. Growing up, I hated needles and would come up with every excuse as to why that particular chosen day would not work out for the busy schedule I had, but, as I should have learned earlier, mom always wins. If I wanted to keep enjoying the amazing food and warm place to stay, I knew I had to eventually give in. As I got older, I began to realize that the sooner you went in, the sooner it was over. This particular year, I surprisingly volunteered to go first, which my sisters were thankful for, since it provided them with a few extra minutes to try to change Mom's mind. The second I got this dreaded moment over with, I sighed a huge sigh of relief and waited in peace for my sisters to get their shots. To me this seemed like a normal year, a normal shot. But little did I know that this tiny needle would impact the rest of my life.

Approximately a month after I got the flu shot, I fell ill with what appeared to be a kidney infection. I went into the doctor, got an antibiotic, felt better, and thought nothing of it! A few months later, however, those same symptoms started coming back. This was very strange for me since I had never had such an infection before. My mom brought me back to the doctor to get another antibiotic. Much to my surprise, a few months later I was back in the doctor's office. I began getting kidney infections more frequently, and they started to become more severe. My physician didn't (seem to) understand why I kept getting these infections, but would just shrug and fill out another prescription. It got to the point that every time I would stop an antibiotic, the infection would come back with a vengeance. Within a few months, I could no longer distinguish between infections- it seemed like one huge infection that would never go away. At this point I began getting discouraged. I wanted to know why this was happening, and no one could seem to give us an answer. I had been to multiple doctors, and basically got the same answer from them all- they were completely stumped. Between doctor appointments, school, and basketball practice, I was so exhausted and in so much pain that when I was at home, I could not get off the couch, but would just lay there- in tears. It wasn't long until I was missing basketball practice, not going to school, and just sleeping on my designated chair, unable to eat or drink much of anything.

My parents were incredibly worried about me. How can any parent stand to watch their oldest daughter in such a state? I will never forget how patient they were with me, and how gentle they were. I remember waking up and hearing them praying the rosary in the kitchen. I would say a Hail Mary under my breath and then I was back asleep.

At this point of my story it was November 2007. It was the night before Thanksgiving and we were getting our final plans together for the family celebrations. We were in charge of bringing the meal for one side of the extended family, so we were making lists and checking groceries. I was laying on my chair feeling incredibly weak when mom and dad tried to get me to eat or drink something but I refused. They ended up bringing me to the emergency room to try to get me hydrated and see if there was anything they could do to relieve some pain. I will never forget watching TV and forcing myself to eat an Eggo waffle on Thanksgiving Day with my dog refusing to leave my lap.

It wasn't too long after Thanksgiving when the doctors did an ultrasound on my kidneys and came to the conclusion that I had Polycystic Kidney Disease. I remember hearing the word 'dialysis' being thrown around and that I had until my early 20s to live. I was oddly at peace with my diagnosis. Maybe I didn't realize how serious it was? But I like to believe I knew God had bigger and better plans, as He always does.

As time went on, there was really no improvement. I wasn't getting any better, but only worse. The next weekend was approaching and my mom had been planning for months for our family to go to the Marian Eucharistic Congress in Fargo, North Dakota. As it was approaching, she asked me how I was feeling and if I thought we could still go as a family. I reluctantly agreed to go because I knew how important it was to her and, after all, mom did give birth to me!

The normal four-hour drive took us twice as long with all the stops we had to make. I was in so much pain and it hurt to sit, stand, lay down, or walk. I would be lying if I said I didn't have an ulterior motive behind going to the conference... Nothing beats a cute Catholic boy! Much to my surprise (and disappointment) my sisters and I were the only "young people" and my parents the next youngest by many years. I am sure God had a good laugh at us as we scanned the bleachers!

The conference was amazing. Words cannot describe how much I enjoyed it, even without any cute Catholic boys! One of the speakers that really stood out to me was Immaculée Ilibagiza as she told her story of surviving the Rwandan genocide and how she attributed her survival to Our Lady. I had a chance to speak with Immaculée and I remember being in such awe of the power of God and how His plans for her were so much bigger than she could have imagined.

The last morning of the conference, October 12, 2008, I was in more pain than I had been the whole weekend. I was overall just exhausted by the whole weekend, as wonderful as it was. I asked my mom if we could leave early as there was *just* Adoration left before the conclusion of the conference. My mom, naturally, really wanted to go to Adoration and convinced me that we should stay just for about 10 minutes.

As we took our seats in the middle of the arena, I had no idea that this was not a typical Adoration hour. The priest started explaining that the Holy Spirit speaks to him and that the Holy Spirit heals people through him. I had never heard of such a thing, but I was all ears since I had always had a fascination for stories like this growing up. This priest then went on to say that today, during this time of Adoration, he was going to list the people who were going to be healed that had been shown to him earlier in his time of prayer before the Blessed Sacrament. He then went on to say that even though he had names, he was only going to say what the person would be healed of, *as it takes faith.*

At this point I still had no idea what was coming. I was still trying to wrap my mind around these miracles being possible when the priest brought out the Monstrance and everyone hit their knees. Before I knew it, the priest was listing problems that- let's face it-a lot of our older population deals with. There were cataracts, hip issues and so much more that would be healed. When the priest got about 2/3 of the way down the list, he spoke the words I never thought I would ever hear him say:

"A young girl is going to be healed of a kidney ailment."

Instantly my whole family started bawling. We were all on our knees, hugging and crying. To this day, it's one of my most treasured memories with my family and one of the first times I remember seeing my father cry.

I will never forget the peace and warmth I felt in my heart the moment the priest lifted the monstrance in the dark room. The incense made the monstrance look almost like a dream as the spotlight made it the focal point. I was not convinced I was awake and actually experiencing such a profound moment.

Needless to say, we stayed in Adoration the entire time, and not just the ten minutes like I had originally planned. When we left the conference, my head was still spinning, and I was trying to figure out if what just happened was actually real. Maybe I had just fallen asleep for a brief moment and had a bizarre dream. I will never forget my little sister, Briana, jumping around me yelling, "How do you feel?! HOW DO YOU FEEL?!"

When we drove the entire four hours home without stopping, it started to hit me- I was healed. When I woke up from a restful and good night's sleep, I became more and more grateful that I was not wincing in pain and could eat breakfast with a big appetite. I think the moment that it hit me the hardest is when we received the letter from the hospital stating what time to be there and to hear my mom call them and tell them we were not coming.

I still have the email I sent to Bishop Aquila after the conference. He had asked any of us who had a powerful experience to write to him.

Most Reverend Bishop Aquila,
I would like to share what a life changing experience the Marian Eucharistic Congress was for me.
I am 17 and was healthy for the majority of my life. Last year after my family received the flu shot we all started getting weird things like bladder and kidney infections. Theirs eventually went away, but I continued getting kidney infections. By September I was getting so sick that I was at the doctor constantly. They normally gave me really strong medicine and as soon as I was off it a day, it would come back. Eventually, I was diagnosed with Polycystic Kidney Disease. About a month later my family went to the Marian Eucharistic Congress. My kidneys were bothering me so bad that we were actually considering leaving before the healing service. Thankfully we stayed and I believe I was healed. On the way to Fargo (from St. Cloud MN) we had to stop numerous times because I couldn't sit. On the way home we did not stop once because I was feeling so great! To this day, I have not had any problems with my kidneys. When we got home from this weekend, we got a letter saying the day I would be admitted to the hospital. I was so excited we could call and say I was no longer in need of that kind of attention!
I would like to thank you for everything you did for the Marian Eucharistic Congress!
God bless,
Tricia Walz

Reflecting on my experience with my kidneys, and now being 27 years old, already out-living the original prognosis from the doctors, I am so incredibly grateful for the mercy He showed to me.

* * *

Needless to say, God healing my kidneys was a huge turning point in my Faith life; but the seed was planted just a couple years earlier.

My entire family was a bit late to the game, so to speak. My mom was the first to have her conversion and my dad quickly followed suit. Once my parents started to get more involved in church activities, they began sending my sisters and I on retreats and to other events to learn more about our rich Catholic Faith.

The first retreat I went on-after which I knew life would never be the same-was the Steubenville Youth Conference. We joined a group that went down to St. Louis and words cannot describe how amazing of an experience it was. The talks were captivating and the music from the heart. I had never been in such a large place that was filled with Catholic high school students. My mom and sister, Nikki, were on this retreat with me and until this point Nikki and I really had our differences. Like many sisters, we fought and said things we didn't mean, so our mom was hoping this retreat would be beneficial for our relationship. Little did she know it was going to do just that and so much more.

On Saturday night of the Steubenville retreat, there are a couple hours of Adoration. Thousands of high school students all on their knees, praying and adoring Jesus Christ, was one of the coolest things I have ever experienced. Assuming the devil knew what good was going to come out of these few hours, he was working as hard as possible to try to scare my sister and I and keep us from encountering Jesus' love and mercy. It was not until this weekend that I truly realized how real the devil is and how he works on every individual in a unique way to try to get them to turn their back on God. During Adoration I would continually get distracted by what appeared to be snakes at the front of the stage in the curtains. When I would stare at the monstrance I felt an overwhelming sense of peace, but when I would look at the snakes I would feel incredibly uneasy. It was as if there was a battle going on inside of me. After Adoration, we all went back to the dorms where we were told to head to bed. Nikki and I both had some strange encounters during Adoration and were a little afraid to go to bed. After assuring each other we were fine and that we should get some sleep, we still decided to go to sleep- but in the same bed of course. At the exact same time, a couple minutes after we said our final 'goodnights,' we both gasped and sat up in terror. Comparing notes, we had both seen the exact same image of Jesus that suddenly turned into the devil. He was the scariest-looking creature I have ever seen.

Terrified, my sister and I ran next door to my mom's room in tears. We told her what had happened and I will never forget how calm she was. She told us to grab a seat on the floor and she handed both of us a rosary. She told us to ask Mary to protect us and not to let the devil take away our peace. This was hands-down the most powerful rosary I have prayed to date. All of the uneasy, scared feelings I had decreased by magnitudes as each Hail Mary was recited. After we finished praying, we went back to our room in a calm state and fell asleep instantly with no bad dreams.

It was on this weekend that I gained a lot of the tools I would need as the future unfolded. God and the devil both became so real to me on that weekend and I knew how much bigger the Catholic Faith was than I ever could have imagined. I also was given a true sense of peace that I would need in the years to come.

* * *

It was these events that solidified my belief in God and His church and helped me make my Faith my own. By this time in my life I was becoming more involved in my youth group, helping in church, and literally had a list of things I wanted to do to change the world (many of my ideas would render a good chuckle and 'good luck' from people I told).

For seven years I kept my experience with my kidneys to myself and my closest family/friends. I felt like if I shared it with too many people, it would almost be considered bragging. I struggled back and forth with these feelings and knew I wanted to consult a priest but the opportunity never presented itself. Seven years later (of course, the *perfect* amount of time), my sisters and I had the life-changing opportunity to go to World Youth Day in Kraków, Poland. This trip changed my life in way more ways than one. It was on the street in Kraków, the stomping grounds of Pope John Paul II and where St. Faustina received visions of Our Lord, that I would finally get a chance to confide in someone about my experiences.

Fr. Russell Kovash was one of the priests with our group. It was my first time ever meeting him, but I knew immediately that he would be the priest I could talk to. We were in the middle of one of our 3-4 mile walks in Poland when we were walking together and I asked him if I could tell him something I had really been struggling with and get his opinion. He listened intently to everything and his advice was something I will never forget. He told me very confidently that God wanted me to share my story and that He wants everyone to share their own story because we have so much to learn from each other.

As I reflected on what Fr. Russell told me, I realized just how true that is. We all have such unique experiences, and I realized just how inspired I feel when I hear someone else's testimony, so why not share mine?

The next day, our group was waiting for our bus to pick us up from our hotel and Fr. Russell came over and sat down next to me. We normally spent the time on the bus praying the Liturgy of the Hours or learning facts about the places we would be seeing that day, but Fr. Russell said he thought it was a good day for a testimony and asked what I thought. So I shared my testimony to the bus full of our new friends, which was a really powerful experience for me. My eyes were opened when multiple people came up to me after the bus ride to tell me about experiences they had, which was incredibly inspiring and confirmed to me the necessity of sharing our stories of God working in our lives.

The last day of World Youth Day we spent outside in a giant field with 2.5 million other young Catholics. Pope Francis came and had a prayer service with us and we had praise and worship until late into the night; then we slept outside with whatever we could carry on our 7-mile hike there. This experience was super powerful for me spiritually. It was in the field that I decided I needed to write down my testimony and share it. When I got back home to the United States, I started asking a couple friends for their testimonies and I was truly blown away. It was then that God changed my plan and asked me to gather testimonies of how other people have also seen God's mercy in their lives. I challenge each of you reading these stories to think of how you have seen God's mercy in your life and to not be afraid to share it. Your story matters and the world needs to hear it!

Leah Wienhold

"My past, O Lord, to Your mercy; my present, to Your love; my future to Your providence."

-St. Padre Pio

When I became pregnant in 2010, it was the end of the world for me. I thought, How could God (if He even exists) allow this to happen, knowing about all the dreams I have for a singing career? I took the easy way (or so I thought) and had an abortion, making sure not to utter a single word about my pregnancy to my devout Catholic family.

Fast-forward to 2012: My oldest sister, Sarah was diagnosed with Stage III breast cancer. Again, it was the end of the world. It was then that I started to seriously question the existence of God. I created the password "Finding God" for Sarah's Caring Bridge website. Boy did God ever answer me! My faith (or lack thereof) was tested during the last few months of my sister's life on this earth. I now lovingly refer to this time as "God's boot camp". Sarah was experiencing what the local Catholic priest explained as spiritual warfare, which my family and I were witness to in my parents' house in St. Cloud, Minnesota. It was both the most terrifying and uplifting time of my life. Satan and his minions were undoubtedly doing their best to pull us away (especially dear Sarah) from the truth and the life, but God, merciful as always, saw to it that we be protected in His warm, loving embrace through those cold winter nights in the Advent season of 2014.

During this special time, God revealed His presence and unconditional love for me, and He continued to reveal it as my sister lay on her deathbed. Having received deliverance prayers and last rites from the priest, Sarah was in a state of grace during her final moments. I vividly remember taking her hand as family members, friends and the priest gathered around her bed. Her eyes were gazing off into another world, and as I held her hand, Sarah said in a low, raspy voice, "She has a son...I can see his face." Instantly I knew she was talking about the baby I had aborted five years prior. My heart raced as I sat in complete, stunned silence. God revealed to her a secret I had kept inside for so many years, a secret which I now share with everyone in hopes of directing this sinful world to the truth that is Christ, our everlasting Savior.

A few months after Sarah's passing, I received the gift of God's forgiveness, followed by my own forgiveness at a Catholic church in Pasadena, California. The Holy Spirit prompted tears of joy the entire

Mass, and the people sitting next to me were probably wondering if I would need to be carried out of the church. I sprinted to confession and happily started my brand new life in God's healing grace.

As I look back throughout the years, I realize I had been set on "finding God" during times of crises, but it was actually God who found me. He picked me up when I was lost and weary and wrapped me up in His tender arms. I was just too blind to see His stunning brilliance and too deaf to hear His gentle whispers while He knocked patiently on my door. Now it is up to me to continue seeing and hearing with my new eyes and new heart all of the plans He has for my life. God has called me out of the darkness and into the light...

Through my conversion, when I realized that Jesus indeed walked the earth, suffered and died on the cross to forgive even the greatest of sinners, it was like the most miraculous fairytale had come true. During the spiritual battle at my childhood home, the rosary in particular helped draw me back to the Catholic Faith. Since then, I have fallen in love with the Faith and have a great thirst for deepening my understanding of it. Having attended and later volunteering at several Rachel's Vineyard retreats, I was able to find further peace, healing and forgiveness.

Today I continue to pray to God and for others, and I listen to Him as He reveals His marvelous plan for my life. I'm eternally grateful for my faithful parents' wisdom, guidance and unconditional love, for my sister, Sarah, and for my son, Abel. I feel comforted knowing that he is "abel" to be with Sarah and Jesus in Heaven.

Sally Traut

"Spread love everywhere you go. Let no one ever come to you without leaving happier."

-St. Mother Teresa

Growing up with siblings can be a beautiful blessing, and for me, this was definitely the case. I grew up with a brother, Samuel, who was three years older than me. Living in the country, there was always lots of work to be done. He and I did everything together: working in the garden, cutting wood, shoveling snow, playing games, working in the kitchen, going on bike rides, helping my dad in his shop, or just simply being. My brother was my best friend, my confidant, and my role model. I valued his opinion and advice above that of anyone else because I knew he understood me and had my best interest in mind. When he went to North Dakota State University for college, I missed him deeply, but our close friendship continued. From the time he left home in August, to when he returned for Thanksgiving, I witnessed a powerful transformation in him. Upon arriving home for break, I could sense this deep, spiritual aura of holiness within him that I had never before felt in a person. I greatly admired and respected him for that, and I knew the Newman Center had a role in this growth. This made me all the more excited and hopeful for when I would go off to college and would be able to participate in religious activities at a Newman Center. When my college years began, I did just that and became involved in the Newman Center at St. Cloud State. I continued to use my brother as my role model and guide as we shared college adventures together, with him visiting me on my campus and I visiting him at his. Shortly after my junior year of college, I remember going on a run and being utterly grateful to God for the amazing life I had been blessed with and for the wonderful friendships that filled my life.

Unfortunately, it's also amazing how quickly your life can change. For me, this day was Tuesday, June 23, 2015. I was working at a summer program for kids when my world as I knew it came crashing down on me. I was outside with a group of kids when I saw a police car pull up to the school. I didn't think much of it since there was a student whose father was a police officer, but the car seemed to be moving oddly slow and didn't park in the parking lot. Shortly after, I was called over the walkie talkie to come to our staff office. I was trying to wrap up the activity I was doing with the kids and get them ready for lunch which took a little bit of time, so I ended up being called a second time. By that time I was wondering, '*What did I do?*

Is there a reason the police car came? Could it be something to do with me?' My mind was starting to churn, but I couldn't come up with anything.

Eventually I got to the office and knew it definitely had something to do with me. There was my mom, red-eyed, with the saddest look I have ever seen on her, standing with a police officer and another man. Before a single word was even said, I knew it was one of two things: either my brother or my dad had suffered a tragedy. My dad was a farm mechanic, so that could definitely have been plausible. My brother had just returned from participating in an evangelization mission trip in Peru, and we had a wonderful weekend with him at home just two days prior, before he returned to Fargo where he worked as a civil engineer. I couldn't think how something could have happened to him, and I was trying to wrack my brain thinking there has to be a mistake. Before saying anything about what happened, the police officer said I should grab my things. Now I really knew something was serious.

The police officer, my mom, the other man, and I were then taken to another room. That was when I heard the news. Samuel, my brother, my best friend, and my role model was murdered in his home the night before. I could not believe it. How could someone so full of life, so committed to God, so generous toward others be taken from this world in such an unfair and disgraceful manner? News like this is something no one can ever be prepared to hear. I kept pleading with God that this has to be a mistake or a dream that will eventually end. The drive home was incredibly difficult. The car my brother had once driven was now passed down to me, so everything I touched and everywhere I looked filled me with memories of when he had once driven me around in that car. It's incredible how the simplest things that never will be again, like driving in a car with my brother, consume your mind in times like this.

The next few days were ones filled with a whirlwind of activities you never want to have to experience: traveling to Fargo to meet with investigators, moving my brother's belongings out of the house he rented with other young men involved with the NDSU Newman Center, planning a funeral, and facing the cold hard truth that he is never coming back. Yet even in these darkest of days, God does not let us forget His presence if we are open to receiving that message.

That message of His grace came to me in a remarkable way. For the first couple of days after hearing the news, I could not bear the thought of eating any food. My body was physically in pain, one like I had never experienced before. Food was the last thing on my mind. I never knew the role one's heartache can play in one's health. Eventually, I knew I needed to try eating something. We had brought back the fresh groceries my brother had just purchased, and one of the items was a loaf of bread. I felt I should start eating again with something basic, like bread. I really didn't want much, so I told myself, '*I'll just take half a piece of bread.*' I opened the bread bag, and shockingly, there was a half piece of bread, torn by my brother just days before. I could not get over this because never before had I ever seen my brother eat just a half piece of bread. It was not like him at all. I choked down tears as I ate that slice of bread, thinking in my head that my brother wanted to share one last meal with me. I savored that meal of bread and never wanted it to end. When I was at Mass a few days later, I felt God telling me the real meaning behind that experience. The host I received that day was a piece that had been broken from the larger host that was elevated during consecration. When I saw that broken host placed in my hand, I had a flashback to the broken slice of bread from a few days prior. Everything suddenly made so much sense. That connection I had of sharing one last meal with my brother through the slice of bread can be felt every time I receive the Eucharist through the Communion of Saints. This left me with such a strong sense of comfort and a deeper appreciation for the beauty of this Sacrament, the Bread of Life. While the earthly sharing in of meals with my brother can no longer happen, I can still spiritually share in a meal with him through the Eucharist.

I am incredibly grateful for this experience. Not only did it remind me of my brother's continual presence in my life, but it made the power of the Eucharist evident to me. With many young people falling away from the Catholic faith, or any faith in general, I am now forever convinced of its truth. This experience eliminated and prevented any potential doubts that could affect my faith. I know what I felt, and I felt such peace in that moment, that I don't ever want to prevent myself from experiencing that.

My brother has always had such a deep level of care for me, even deeper than I had known. After his death, many of his friends approached me saying that he always referred to me as his "Number One Girl." Another friend of his mentioned that while on the mission trip in Peru, Sam was always on the lookout for something special to get for me. I had no idea how much of a part of his life I was, and I was beyond humbled to hear these words. Knowing how he lived his earthly life with so much concern for me, I came to understand that he would continue to do so in the next life. His friends said I now have the best intercessor in heaven. Seeing how he made that Eucharistic connection so powerful for me, I know Sam will continue to guide me as I follow the path of God. While it could be so easy for me to become angry at God for taking my best friend from me, I know God puts certain people in our lives for a reason, and Sam definitely was and continues to be a key factor in mine. It's comforting to know that God's gift of grace can shine through in even the darkest of times.

Fr. Doug Liebsch

*"By the grace of God I am what I am,
and his grace to me has not been ineffective."*

-1 Corinthians 15:10

I was asked to give a testimony. The word testimony itself refers to *evidence* or *assertion* of something. And so as simple as it may be I submit my evidence and assertion that God is alive and active in my life.

I grew up knowing that God was real and had a plan for my life. I remember stories my parents told us. I would like to begin by sharing one of those. When I was young my parents were like many newly-weds living in rural MN. They were living paycheck to paycheck, eating a lot of venison and potatoes, and cutting out any financial expenses that were not absolutely essential. Before my first birthday, they (meaning my dad) felt God calling them to tithe. In tithing we seek to realize the simple fact that everything we have is God's. In Malachi we hear the words, "Bring the whole tithe into the storehouse...Put me to the test says the Lord of hosts, And see if I do not open the floodgates of heaven for you, and *pour down upon you blessing without measure.*" However appealing that may sound, tithing is a difficult thing to live. My Dad simply thought that tithing was the thing that needed to happen as his young family desired to put their trust in God. This wasn't going over so well with my mom. One thing that was not absolutely essential in my life up until that point was a pair of shoes. In my first year I hadn't started walking yet and during summer shoes weren't necessary either; but as I was spending more time on my feet and the weather in Minnesota was turning from summer to winter, shoes became more essential. Of course my parents could have found a pair for $10, but of all the decisions they made that week, the last one came down to choosing a pair of shoes for their son approaching his first birthday or choosing to tithe.

At the end of the week they put their tithe in the Church envelope and headed to Mass. My mom was very conscious of the money that was currently in the envelope and soon to be gone in the collection basket. She saw the basket go by my dad as he put the money in, and as it went by her she felt the urge to reach in and take it out again. Instead she held herself back and turned to the Presence of Jesus in the tabernacle with a sense of trust, and with a tone of demand in her heart said, "You have to take care of us now." God stays true to His promise. My parents did not tell anybody about their recent decision and somewhat embarrassing struggle to come up with a few dollars for a pair of shoes. That didn't stop God from sending one of His own about a week later to park in the driveway and drop off a few things, including not just one, or two, but 13 pairs of shoes! The floodgates of heaven were indeed *poured down upon us without measure.* Through the objective lens this was a simple thing, but a true sign of God's Providential care.

Hearing stories like this as a young boy helped me know that God was very active. I know this won't happen every time, but reflecting on them now helps me remember that our Father is always one to be trusted.

With that being said it seems that my whole life is a process of God asking me to trust Him more. This came into play more concretely as I was thinking about plans after high school. The seminary was something that had been on my mind for a while. My senior year of high school I met with the vocations director. I guess I was expecting him to tell me to sign up for seminary or at least say it would be a good thing if I did. He never said anything like that and left the ball in my court completely. I wasn't convinced I should enter seminary, so I decided to go to NDSU and pursue a major in civil engineering. My mom knew that even though I was heading to college, the seminary was still a possibility. Before I left she simply said that God would let me know and the only thing that would prevent me from hearing His voice would be sin.

Entering college, I knew my faith was something very important to me. In the first few weeks I readily signed up for a Bible Study through St. Paul's Newman Center. Through the connections and friendships I made there God continued to work. I heard of this weekend retreat coming up at Cardinal Muench Seminary that at that time was open in Fargo, ND. I signed up without thinking too much about it. On the way there I learned that this perhaps was less of a typical retreat and more of a time for guys to come and check out the seminary. That was ok with me, but I was a little confused why the friend presenting this to me didn't explain this to me before…

I showed up and I am sure we played a lot of games, heard some nice talks and said some prayers. That evening I received one of the most powerful God moments in my life. It had been some time since I went to confession. As Catholics of course this is where we believe God the Father forgives our sins through the Priesthood of His Son, Jesus Christ, which the priest participates in. I knew this of course and approached this sacrament with faith. After I expressed the sins on my heart the priest gave me penance and communicated the forgiveness of God through the prayer of absolution. I was confessing through the screen. As the priest said the words of pardon, I remember looking up and at the same time something touched my soul. It was not only the normal peace I had often felt after going to confession many times growing up. This time there was a warmth that touched the deepest part of me and at the same time a deep knowledge that I was going to be a priest. I was convinced to the depths of my being that the priesthood was what God was calling me to in this life. I cannot really describe that powerful moment. In my soul there was a movement of surrender to that call. As much as the priesthood scared me, in that moment there was no fear. I just felt very at peace with myself and who God created me to be. In reflection on that time I often think of those words my mom spoke to me before I left. It was in the moment where there was no sin on my soul where I became acutely aware of God's plan for my life.

After the retreat was finished, the grace and trust in God already seemed to be waning. As much as I profoundly knew of God's plan, I didn't want myself to fully admit it. One evening a few weeks later I emailed the vocations director. I let him know I was interested in applying to the seminary, but not yet fully committed. The next day, I received a packet in the mail from him with a little note: "Hey Doug, I have been thinking of you and haven't heard from you in a while. Here is an application packet..." I was surprised because I knew he wouldn't have been able to send the packet in time after receiving my email, as his note implied. I was very reassured that this was something from God. Unsolicited he simply volunteered the packet at the same time I was asking for it!

As I finished up my one and only year at NDSU, I headed down to St. Cloud for my interview with the Bishop for the seminary. I was a little behind schedule as I hit the road. God not only provided, but literally continued to open the path before me as I drove through St.

Joseph, Waite Park, and St. Cloud...I didn't have to stop for a red light the whole way down, through 17 stoplights! It really was God giving me the green light. In my own weakness I continued to need that reassurance.

I entered the seminary and continued on until I was ordained a priest 7 years later. During the journey I continued to question God as I do many times even now. However, despite my own unworthiness, Our Heavenly Father continues to pour down upon me blessing without measure.

Amanda and Jessica Vasek

"I urge you to live in a manner worthy of the call you have received, with all humility and gentleness, with patience, bearing with one another through love."

-Ephesians 4:1-2

Growing up, our family would go to Sunday Mass most weekends. Many Sundays we tried avoiding Mass by "sleeping in" a little extra, never reminding our parents it was a Sunday, or having sleepovers Saturday nights. Mass was not something that we enjoyed going to, but we knew that we had to. Our parents told us that Religion was important and spending time with God in prayer was encouraged. We did not truly know how critical our Faith was until after our brother was born.

On September 26th, 2005, our family gained its newest member; our little brother, Logan, was born. Our whole family could not have been more excited. Our father, Shane, was ecstatic that we would finally have a hockey player in the family and we as sisters were excited to be taking care of a real baby instead of a baby doll. Amanda was eight years old, Jessica was seven, and Megan was two years old. We enjoyed having our mother, Karla, home for the weeks after Logan was born. She would drive us to school and have the best snacks ready for us when we came off the bus. It was such a treat. We did not have a care in the world.

Two months later, Logan went in to the doctor for a regular check-up. What our parents did not tell us was that Logan had not been eating well, so they were very anxious to talk to the doctor about this. At his appointment, they found out that he weighed five ounces less than when he was born. Our family doctor immediately knew something was wrong so he admitted Logan to the St. Cloud Hospital. Throughout the next couple of days, Logan had many tests on him to see if they could figure out what was wrong. It felt like forever just to discover what the root of this could be. Eventually, the St. Cloud Hospital identified that he had two holes in his heart, and his aorta was very narrow, known as Ventricular Septal Defect (VSD) and Coarctation of the Aorta. The hospital thought it would be best if they sent him to Fairview University Hospital in Minneapolis, Minnesota. Logan was transported to Fairview by ambulance and they confirmed what the St. Cloud Hospital detected. At this time we were pretty confused. We were told that we were supposed to pack a suitcase and that we were going to be staying at our cousins' house for a while. For the first couple days it was fun. Our uncle never failed to put a smile on our face before serving breakfast and driving us to school. We got to hang out with our cousins and enjoyed playing with their dog. Our parents told us to pray for Logan, and while staying at our cousins' house, they continued taking us to Mass every weekend. At this point, nothing more than a few words to God were spoken asking for healing for our brother every once in a while. We had not yet been struck by the power of prayer or been able to grasp the fact that prayer has the ability to change concrete situations.

In less than one week, life went from being "normal" to the start of the craziest days of our lives. Logan had his first open heart surgery to fix the coarctation of the aorta. He went into surgery at 8:45am and did not get out until 4:30pm. He was then put on a ventilator and went into the ICU to recover. When they took the ventilator out a couple days later, they realized that Logan's voice was gone.

It was really hard on our parents to be away from the rest of us kids and to see their two-month-old son in so much pain. They still did their best to make sure that everyone was happy. My parents made a CaringBridge website so that they could update all of their friends and family all at once. While making the site, they had not realized until later on that it was a great way for people to support them while they were many miles away from home. This support helped them a lot to get through the lonely days of sitting in a hospital without the rest of the family or company.

When Logan got out of the ICU, he still was not eating very well. A doctor checked up on him and realized that his left vocal cord was paralyzed. The doctor informed our parents that it could be a month or two before he would get his voice back. Our parents continued to ask people for their prayers so that Logan would have a good recovery. Not only did family and friends pray for Logan, but also strangers that we had never met. About a week after Logan got out of the ICU, he was readmitted to it. He was not eating and would sometimes cry uncontrollably. The only way to get him to settle down was to give him medication.

A month into this journey, out parents finally came home for a night. Being at the hospital for such a long time was mentally draining for them. Dad still worked, so even though he was not at the hospital every night, that did not mean that we would always get to see him. When they went back to the hospital, they stopped at a Chinese restaurant. They opened their fortune cookies and one of them said "The trouble is past and the future from now on is brighter." They normally would just eat the cookie and throw the fortune away, but this time they really needed hope, so they saved the fortune hoping it would be true.

Our parents stayed at the hospital until Christmas Eve night, then came back home for Christmas. It was hard leaving Logan alone around the holidays, but they also knew that it was important to make it a special day for us girls. They went back to the hospital the next day, and we went back at our cousins' house. After Christmas, Logan got a feeding tube so that he would be able to get all of the nutrients that he needed. Our parents came back home to celebrate New Year's Eve. It was good for them to get out of the small hospital room and be around family and friends. The feeding tube had only been in for a few days, but it was helping Logan gain some weight. You could tell just by looking at him that he was weighing more.

On January 7th, 2006, Logan finally got to come back home! Everything was looking better for Logan. My parents wanted to be prepared for when they took Logan home, so they took a class on how to give CPR and how to use the feeding tube. All of my grandparents and some of the aunts also took the class for extra caution. Our house finally felt like a home again. Logan was taking eight medications a day, but all we cared about was being all together as a family. We went back to living life as normal; we went to school and would come back home to a yummy snack that our mother would make. We did not tell many people at school what was going on because it was hard for us to understand what was happening ourselves. A nurse would come to our house every once-in-awhile to make sure Logan was still as healthy as he could be. I remember when we got to come home and attend Sunday Mass at our regular parish, the prayers of the faithful would always include prayers for Logan and we would have so many people coming up to us telling us that they were praying for Logan and our family. The support that we had cheering us on was remarkable; something we were all truly grateful for! What a gift it was to be surrounded by such a loving, supportive, and prayer-filled community.

At the end of January, Logan's feeding tube came out while a home nurse was at our house. Seeing a hole in Logan's abdomen was quite shocking to our mother, so the nurse kept her calm while she called the doctor. The doctor instructed her to get Logan to the St. Cloud Hospital immediately. There was no one at the hospital that could put the tube back in, so they had to go back to U of M Fairview. He had a surgery at 9:00 PM. Since they had to go back to Fairview, Logan missed an appointment with the gastroenterologist. Our parents were extremely frustrated. They would ask anyone who came into the room the next day if they could see the gastroenterologist yet. They were on about three hours of sleep and anyone could have guessed that. Eventually my mother kicked my father out of the hospital because he was taking his frustration out on anyone in a few feet radius. Us girls were back at our cousins' house and now showing signs of separation anxiety. Logan got to come back home a few days later, so that meant we could too. We were all struggling while they were gone, so it felt good to have them home. Logan was doing well for the situation he was in. He was gaining some weight back and even showing us smiles. We were living day-by-day. Simply leaving the hospital and being reunited as a whole family felt so good again.

For the next three months, we got to live at home going to school during the week, attending Mass on the weekend and having family dinners. We were savoring the time because we knew it would not last forever. On April 21st, Jessica received her First Communion. This is an important day in the Church, so many friends and family came to support her. It was weird that, for once in a long while, Logan did not have all the attention.

Four days later, Logan had another surgery to fix the VSDs. After surgery, they noticed that he was in a post-operative state called Junctional Ectopic Tachycardia. This is when the heartbeat is irregular and rapid. Patients normally are in "JET" for 3-4 days but

Logan was in it for six days. After surgery, they put in some chest tubes. When they were about to take them out a few days later, he stopped breathing. My mom was the only one at the hospital, and my dad was on his way. Shane got the phone call from Karla and he started speeding down the highway so that he could get back to them. The doctors were just about to put Logan on the ventilator when he started breathing, so he no longer needed it. Our parents were then informed that three new holes had formed in Logan's heart after the surgery. Logan was a little bit older now, so they thought they could repair it with a scope in his leg rather than having another open-heart surgery.

On May 13th, Amanda's birthday, Logan got to come home from the hospital again. To this day, Amanda will say it was the greatest birthday present she had ever received. Our mother was still off from work. Thanks to her employer, they had given her more time off. Our father was still working most days so that we would have an income. Logan started seeing a speech therapist who would eventually get him to eat orally. She would come to our house two times a week. Logan was becoming healthier by the day, and we were grateful that we could hold our brother. A few months later, the cardiologist confirmed that the holes in Logan's heart were starting to heal by themselves. The holes were getting smaller, so they did not need to operate on him again.

In mid-September of 2006 Logan had an appointment with Ear Nose and Throat, and they discovered that his left vocal cord was still paralyzed. The doctors said by this time it probably would not heal on its own, but they still wanted to wait a year before doing anything unless he showed signs of pain. My parents asked if Logan would ever be able to play sports, and the doctor replied that if things did not improve by themselves, then Logan would have trouble walking up a flight of stairs without being out of breath. This was not what they wanted to hear and made them realize how serious it really was. But, to our surprise, Logan went from taking ten heart medications three times a day to taking zero heart medications in just two months! His heart was looking good. Logan was in physical, occupational and speech therapy twice a week. He was still having some problems eating by mouth, but it got better with time.

June 2007, Logan's left vocal cord began working again, and a few months later his heart was fully healed and his feeding tube was removed. These were all huge leaps of healing for him and each one was celebrated. Today, Logan is an active thirteen year old. He is currently in 7th grade and loves school. He is in hockey, soccer, and plays cello, and piano. His love for sports also encouraged him to try baseball, lacrosse and football. Looking at him now, you never would have guessed his past aside from a few scars. He brings so much joy and laughter to our family. As a young girl, Amanda spent so many of her coins tossed into a wishing well asking and praying to God for a brother, and wow! God gave us the biggest blessing and a human being that is loved so much. Logan is a constant reminder of the amazing miracles in this world.

Going through the Caring Bridge website that our parents wrote, we have noticed that at the end of every post, they would ask for the people reading to pray for Logan and others who were in the hospital. Also, when they would post, it was not always just about Logan. They would wish others a Merry Christmas or safe travels. On random weekends they would wish for others to have good days. If a friend or family member was having health problems or needed prayers, our parents would post it on CaringBridge and ask to share Logan's prayers with others who needed them as well. This shows us that life is not always about ourselves. There are so many who struggle in this world, so it is so crucial to take the time to pray for others.

Throughout the whole time that we stayed at our cousin's house, they supported our faith and took us to Mass every weekend. Our parents would also go to the hospital chapel to pray and go to Mass. Although we did not know how important it was to pray for Logan at the time, a great number of family and friends did and that is what got my parents through, knowing God's love and support. Looking back at our experience, we have learned that God was with all of us and answering all of the prayers being said for Logan. After a few years of growing in our faith, we realized that it was not by luck that our brother, Logan, is still with us today; it was through God and all the graces he had been working in our lives.

God gave our parents the strength to be brave and strong for us. Even though they were undoubtedly living some of the worst months of their lives, they were still doing everything they could to make sure the rest of us kids were okay. Our mother was a stay-at-home mom, but she was working 24/7 with Logan, and she still took the time to make a little snack for us as we got off the bus. Looking back, it was the little things that made our days. It helped a lot when families would send dinners or would just come over to visit so that my parents could take a break from watching Logan. Although he was a good-looking kid, there were a lot of things to do around the house which they were able to do quickly because the visitors entertained him. Even family from out of state came to visit.

It can be easy to fall on hard times, seeing it as darkness or desolation, and to focus on all of the things that go wrong, but we will miss all of the ways God has been working during these times. The moments that were hardest to make it to Faith Formation classes, Mass or to pray were the times we grew the most. These times can lay the foundation for the faith that continues to flourish throughout the years. It was never God's perfect will that our family had to experience the stress, separation, or sadness while my brother was in the hospital, but He allowed a greater good to come about from these situations. We learned the importance of prayer and a personal relationship with Jesus, as well as how necessary it is to be supportive for people in good and bad times. Everyone is living with struggles and it is a better world when we all work together to make this life easier for each other by our kind gestures and words. Today, our hearts have been set on fire for Him and we have strong relationships with God that have withstood the tests and trials that have come our way. By realizing that God is walking with us during the rainy days and not just when the sun is shining allows us to have a confidence in knowing that we will be able to make it through anything that comes our way.

We feel incredibly blessed to know the love and support that surrounded us then and the people who continue to support us today. Our hearts have been filled with gratitude beyond measure and has made us more aware of the small graces and gifts that God continues to pour down upon each and every one of us.

Nikki Walz

*"My flesh and my heart may fail,
but God is the strength of my heart
and my portion forever."*

-Psalm 73:26

In a little box of treasured possessions I keep in my room, there's a rock and a folded-up letter on notebook paper addressed to God, in my best 12-year-old handwriting. I have to laugh looking back at it now, but it was the first profound experience I had of God, and it all started with a rock. Yep, that's right: a rock. I was raised Catholic, went to Catholic school and then Faith Formation classes when I began public school, and my family went to Mass nearly every Sunday. You would think that I had it all together and that I would have had a deep relationship with God by that point, but my relationship with God was almost completely exterior, and very superficial. I hadn't yet experienced God's presence in a real, tangible way, even though I received Him in the Eucharist every week. On this particular day, I was helping with outside duty at my mom's daycare, and I stumbled upon a rock in our backyard that looked exactly like a silhouette of our Blessed Mother Mary holding baby Jesus. It was such an ordinary thing, but it felt anything but ordinary—I was stopped dead in my tracks, and I just felt an overwhelming sense of God's nearness and that He wanted my attention. I ran inside and grabbed a pen and paper, and I wrote a letter to Him. Where those words came from I have no idea, but reading them now, I know that God was preparing my heart for His in a way that I never could have imagined.

> *Dear God,*
> *I love You with all my heart, soul, and mind. I promise, from this day forward, to follow Your commandments, to pray to You every day at least twice, and to do a good deed for someone else every day. Let this rock be a symbol of my commitment and our covenant with each other. I'm very sorry for not being that close with You over the past 11 years. But I <u>promise</u> to try my hardest to become as close as possible to You over the rest of my life. I love You, Lord. You are my Savior, and You will always be.*
> *Love Forever,*
> *Nicole Walz*

It's amazing to look back and see that as much as I wanted to find God and draw close to Him, *He* was the One Who was pursuing my heart and was constantly seeking me, but never in the ways that I expected. When I was 13, both of my parents had a powerful conversion and began to learn and teach my sisters and I the Faith for the first time, since they had never really learned their faith and had become lukewarm. Soon after, my younger sister Briana got very sick with acid reflux that aspirated to her lungs and caused permanent lung damage, and it became so severe that she couldn't go to school anymore because she couldn't walk from class to class. My mom was left with no choice but to homeschool her, which was a bit of a daunting task while taking care of a daycare of ten kids at the same time! She found a Catholic program called Seton Home Study, based out of Front Royal, VA, and soon my older sister Tricia started asking to be homeschooled. My mom began to think about homeschooling all three of us, but I was 110% against the idea since I had some very negative preconceptions of what homeschooling was and had the usual teenage fears of not having any friends, not being able to see the cute boy in my class every day, and being "weird." Somehow, by the grace of God, I woke up one morning and told my mom I was ready to do it—I know it must have taken the prayers of all the saints to guide me to make that decision, because I definitely wouldn't have done it on my own! When we all began to be homeschooled at the start of my sophomore year of high school, I began to really learn about the richness of our Catholic Faith for the first time, and I was captivated by it. I couldn't believe that I had never known most of these things, or maybe I was just too closed off to receive it before, but my eyes were being continually opened to the beauty that was there all along.

I could talk all day about the powerful ways God was working in my life in high school, but I'll just briefly say that during my sophomore year, I went to a Steubenville Conference and experienced God's love and power in a profound way, then went on a nun-run (against my will) and God opened my heart to discerning the religious life for the first time and also led me to meet my best friend who discerned with me and joined the Nashville Dominicans right out of high school, a friendship for which I will be eternally grateful! By the end of my senior year, I had discerned that God was not calling me to the religious life (even though I had gone from hating the idea to wanting to be His bride so much), and I knew without a doubt that I wanted to study Theology and continue to learn more about God and

His Church so that I could love Him more and more. At the same time, I was very sick with acid reflux that aspirated into my sinuses, which got to the point that I could barely eat anything, and during the summer after my senior year I had to have the same serious surgery that my sister had previously had, where they created a new valve for the top of my stomach. I spent a good majority of my freshman year at Benedictine College in the Emergency Room and doctor's office with complications from the surgery. God was teaching me so much about the meaning and beauty of suffering through my experiences during that time, while helping me to continually pursue His truth through studying Theology.

But God was doing even more in my life than I realized at the time. Little did I know that one of my close friends from freshman year, Ben, would be someone God would use to show me His mercy in one of the most unexpected and difficult ways. (Ben's real name is Brian, but he introduced himself to my group of friends as Ben, a nickname of his from high school, and it stuck.) Our group of friends was inseparable. The guys would go to the 9:30pm daily Mass with us girls and then come hang out in our dorm talking and laughing until the very last second of visitation hours, running out of the dorm before midnight hit. When Ben decided to enter seminary at the end of freshman year, he wrote letters to our group of friends with all sorts of memories we had made together and hid them in bottles all over campus, leaving us clues to decode in order to find them. After freshman year, we went to visit him and kept in touch through Facebook and letters, getting the updates on seminarian life and sharing our excitement with him for the day he'd be ordained a priest.

Then on July 9, 2016, what seemed to be an ordinary Saturday, my world stopped. I got a text from one of my friends who grew up in the same town as Ben, telling us that Ben had gone kayaking that morning with a group of friends on the Arkansas River and had gone missing. One of the girls in their group, Kristen, was pulled underwater when her kayak hit a rough patch of churning water under a bridge. Ben stopped to help her as she was pulled under by the current over and over, giving her a life jacket and pushing her to safety, but then he was pulled under the water himself. That's the last time anyone saw him. After horribly long hours of searching for him, the rescue effort became a recovery effort, and three weeks later, his body was found downstream. Those were some of the most heart-wrenching weeks of my life, but the miracles that came with them completely dumbfounded me.

The day after Ben died, I wrote a blog about him and what had happened, so I could get my raw thoughts and emotions out on paper and to begin to process it all. Within just a few days, the blog had reached over 16,000 people across the country and countless people had been touched by Ben's act of love by giving his life to save a friend. Later I re-read one of the letters he had written and hid in one of the bottles for our friend group to find, and I immediately got goosebumps when I found this: "At this point in my life, I believe I will become much more than just a priest, that I am called to something higher, enabling me to reach out to thousands of Catholics." And so he had, even more than I think he ever could have imagined.

A few days later, the woman he had saved, Kristen, reached out to me, and I was able to meet her a few months later when I went down to Wichita to see the place where he had died and visit his grave. She told me the details of what had happened, and I was shocked and flooded with peace and the certainty that God had His hand in all of it. She said that she had only met Ben that morning, and right before the accident happened, they were talking about his vocation and what made him decide to become a priest. She later said, "Brian told us that he had always kinda thought he might want to be a priest; but no matter what profession he chose, he knew he wanted to help and serve people. He thought about police and firefighter before deciding that it was as a priest that he was called to help and serve in big, bold ways." We also found his bucket list after his death that he had sent to my friend Anne, and one of his items was to "save someone's life by physically doing something, like a hero." Kristen said that Ben "was completely calm the whole time. There was no tremble in his voice or fear in his eyes. Brian was completely 'in persona Christ' to me in that moment." She said that she also was completely at peace in those moments, even though she knew there was a good chance she wouldn't make it out alive. Every time she would go underwater, her foot would find a rock to be able to spring herself back to the surface for air before going back under, and every time she came up she saw Ben's face, completely calm, reassuring her that everything would be okay. The other seminarian that was kayaking with them had made it to shore and saw a fisherman on the other side of the river who was waving his hands to get his attention and pointing to a spot in the river where Kristen was floating on her back downstream. The seminarian was able to pull her to shore because of the fisherman's direction, but when he looked back the fisherman was gone, and others who were there say that they never saw such a fisherman there. If that's not a proof of God's mercy and the real presence of angels, I don't know what is!

At his funeral, the Bishop of Wichita put it perfectly: "He may not have been a priest, but he lived and died a most priestly life." My prayer and hope is that I can live out my life the way that Ben lived his. I feel so incredibly blessed to have known him and to have such a powerful example to follow! The fall after he passed away, I was leading a Confirmation retreat for about 20 high school boys, and Fr. Doug came up to me right before Mass and asked if I had a safety pin because he had been playing ultimate Frisbee and a button ripped from his collar. I looked through my purse and found the pin that Kristen had given me, with Ben's initials, a crucifix, and John 15:13- "No greater love is there than this: to lay down one's life for a friend." I offered it to Fr. Doug to use and as he wore it to pin together his collar for the Mass, I couldn't help but be struck by the significance of it. Ben was still a priest, even if it was in such a different way than we expected. And I feel confident that he is interceding for young men, seminarians, and priests in a special way.

I've learned that life is never what we expect, but God's grace and mercy are so present even in the darkest of times. The deepest desire of my heart is to continually be drawn closer to God's heart and to live my life for others just as Ben did, in imitation of Jesus. Some of Ben's last words in a letter to our friends are a beacon for me now: "Either way, after all this, my life is simply on a short journey to the everlasting kingdom of God. My time here on earth is short, and so I must make the best of it." I pray we can do the same.

*Update: One of the seminarians made a holy card to encourage people to pray for Ben/Brian's intercession, and there have been numerous instances of miracles relating to infertility through those prayers. If you or someone you know struggles with infertility, or if you have another special intention for which you would like to ask his intercession, below is the prayer. Please let us know if you receive miracles through his intercession! Ben, pray for us!

Lord God, Your servant Brian worked tirelessly for the sake of others, and, through his death, You provide us an example of a man who possessed the same redemptive love that You have for each one of us. Grant that our lives may reflect his sacrificial love, dedicated solely to Your service. And if it be Your will, grant (state petition) through his intercession for Your greater glory and the salvation of souls. Amen.

Fr. Derek Wiechmann

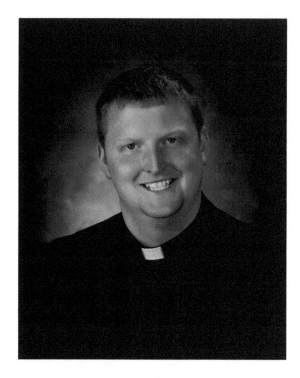

"Therefore I tell you, do not worry about your life, what you will eat or what you will drink, or about your body, what you will wear. Is not life more than food, and the body more than clothing? Look at the birds of the air; they neither sow nor reap nor gather into barns, and yet your heavenly Father feeds them. Are you not of more value than they? And can any of you by worrying add a single hour to your span of life?"

-Matthew 6:25-27

I remember it as though it were yesterday. Every evening, after milking the cows and chores were finished, my family would sit down in the living room and pray a rosary together. Rarely did we miss. Some evenings, well, if I am honest, most evenings I dreaded praying the rosary. I was already tired from the day and often I had homework to do. Mom and Dad insisted, though, and had each one of us (there were 6 children in the family) lead the rosary each night.

Faith was always important growing up. We went to Sunday Mass and often First Friday Mass which was followed by Eucharistic Adoration and confession, always led by a beloved priest, Father Arthur Hoppe. Our farm was located one and a half miles from St. Rosa. It was a quick drive to Church, and it seemed like everyone in the town and in the area was Catholic.

Even with of all this influence it wasn't until I was 13 years old until any of that became important to me. It wasn't until this moment that any of that mattered to me. It wasn't until I first had an encounter with Jesus that I made the faith my own.

I remember this encounter too, as though it just happened yesterday. How could one not remember meeting the love of your life for the first time? Friday evening Mass had finished and Father Hoppe went to expose the Blessed Sacrament on the altar, as he did so many times before. He went to the confessional and people began to get in line. I remember that night being particularly agitated, my soul wasn't at peace. In many ways I didn't want to be there, I had hoped to go to a party with some friends that evening instead. Little did I know what the Lord had prepared for my heart that night.

As Adoration continued, and as I complained to the Lord of the places I would have rather been, the Lord gave me the grace of feeling his presence. It wasn't an experience I had ever had before. It was as though the Church became empty, and Jesus and I were there alone. Together. I was completely at peace. I began to regret and feel sorrow for ever wanted anything but to be with the Lord. It was as though he took my heart that night and has had it ever since. Not many words were shared between him and I, but I knew I wanted to follow him. I wanted to follow Jesus wherever he led me, no matter what.

While my love for Jesus and his Church continued to grow throughout high school, I experienced the usual temptations of anyone else my age. Through these trying years, the Lord kept drawing me closer to himself. His invitation to follow him led me to consider the priesthood. After visiting the seminary, it became evident to me that this was what God wanted. 8 years later, and probably a books worth of stories, I was ordained a priest on June 3rd, 2017.

Hannah Molitor

"The mercy of God, hidden in the Blessed Sacrament, and the voice of the Lord who speaks to us from the throne of mercy: Come to Me, all of you..."

-St. Faustina Kowlaska

My story starts in winter of 2009/2010. I was a college freshman. My day usually started with farm business management class which started at 7:45AM. That was one class you did NOT want to be late for. This one particular Friday, on my journey across the parking lot, I got a phone call from my mom. She and some other women from our parish were organizing a women's conference that was taking place the next day.

The phone call seemed like a typical phone conversation between a mother with a list of things to do and an annoyed 19-year-old daughter who definitely had no time for those things:
"Hannah, on your way home this weekend, can you stop at so and so's house and pick up those cases of waters for tomorrow, then stop at such and such place and grab those flowers and bring all of that to the parish center? Then I need you to be there early tomorrow to light the candles and serve the coffee, and greet the ladies on their way in."
"Yeah, ok Mom. This isn't my first time helping, I know how the process works. And can't someone else pick up the water and flowers? I need to go, I'm going to be late for class!"

Ignoring my pettiness, she continued to chat about her big day the next day. She eventually needed to hang up because she was about to hit the dead spot on the road - because that's what life was like back then on County Road 47 with a Samsung flip phone and T-Mobile service.

A few hours later, I was sitting in class when my phone rang again. It was my sister Leah. We chat on a regular basis, so I casually screened her call with plans to call her later. A few seconds later, my friend Dan who was sitting two seats from me, got a call from Leah. She was due any day with her first child; my parents first grandchild, so obviously everyone in the family was beyond excited and waiting for the big news. I was instantly filled with joy because why else would she try so hard to get in touch with me?

That phone call with Leah on Friday January 29th, 2010 changed my life forever. No, Phillip was not born yet. Instead, I learned my mother, who was on her way to 8AM daily Mass with my youngest two sisters, was killed in a car accident that morning. The car accident happened less than a minute after my conversation with my mom that morning. I was overwhelmed with the shame that potentially her last conversation was with me, a sassy 19-year-old, who had no time.

Days, months and years after my mom's death, our family received an overwhelming amount of love and support from family, friends and strangers. Countless people would reach out to us and tell us their personal story of how my mom had touched their life from prayer, and in a way that they could never repay her. I knew my mom had a powerful prayer life. Praying was her thing, and there was power behind those prayers. The rosary and Eucharistic Adoration were her favorites, and each time she prayed the rosary or went to her holy hour, she had a prayer intention for someone new.

Often, she would bring us with her to Eucharistic Adoration. Eucharistic Adoration became a normal thing for our family growing up. As a kid sitting in Adoration, the only focus going through my mind was the countdown of minutes until the end of the hour. (As an adult now, it is really embarrassing to admit I was *that* kid…).

After college, I moved to small town with a Catholic Church right in the center of town. In that point of my life, it had been years since I had been to Eucharistic Adoration. I started to get this urge to visit an Adoration Chapel. It didn't matter which chapel or church I went to; on numerous occasions, I would walk up to the door of the chapel, attempt to open the door, but then like the backside of a magnet, I would end up completely repelled. Physically, emotionally, nor mentally, I could not walk inside.

One day on my walk to the post office, I again had the urge to attend Adoration. I decided to give it another go. I peacefully walked through the back doors of the church and slid into a random pew. I didn't make it all the way to the Adoration Chapel off to the side; instead, I sat in the main church by myself in silence. After a few minutes, the silence was broken by a women's voice in the Adoration Chapel. She was singing the Divine Praises. I didn't know who she was, and I never will know, but I immediately recognized the voice I heard.

Somehow, for the first time since the morning of January 29, 2010, I heard my own mother's voice singing the Divine Praises. Instantly, I began to sob uncontrollably. It was an unexplainable, exalting, and the most beautiful moment filled with pure love and forgiveness. It was a moment created for me.

Since that day, I truly am filled with the same feeling of love and compassion each time I visit Jesus in Eucharistic Adoration. It is in these moments that I find life to be clear and recharged. Because of this, I give all my praises and thanksgiving to the Holy Spirit for compelling me to stop in that day.

Molly McGowan

"Trust in the LORD with all your heart,
on your own intelligence do not rely;
In all your ways be mindful of him,
and he will make straight your paths."

-Proverbs 3:5-6

I was the kid who was at Mass every Sunday. I went to a Catholic elementary school as well as Catholic high school. Everything was fine until 8th grade; it was then that I started questioning my Faith. There wasn't a specific reason either- I guess there was just so much "Catholic" being thrown at me that I thought it was blinding me from something. "We're sending thoughts and prayers" and "Offer it up for someone who has it worse", felt like a way of making my feelings less valued and real. Beginning in 9th grade, when people would ask me about my Faith I would say I was raised Catholic. If anyone ever says that, they most likely mean "I'm not Catholic anymore but instead of going through that whole story and possibly offending you, I'd rather just mention a religion and move on." Around the middle of freshmen year, I identified as atheist. I remember always being so angry. I was mad at the world because I thought the world was mad at me. That year I had a teacher named Deacon Jim. I stopped in his class and spent many mornings talking with him until the bell rang. That helped me feel less alone. Someone who is Catholic had finally accepted that I wasn't Catholic and actually listened to my opinions and what I had to say. It was refreshing. That summer, my mom had heard about something called Steubenville. She asked if I'd like to go and every time I said no. Why would I want to go to a *Catholic* conference? After a few weeks passed, my mom mentioned that this was the last offer for sign ups. I sighed, said yes, and instantly regretted it.

On the trip we did some service work which was not that bad, more fun than anything. The first day of the conference was nuts. We walked in to take our seats and a band came out onto the stage. They barely even had played their first note before everyone rushed to the stage. Everyone knew the words; they all danced this dance that I had for sure never seen, and I looked around only to realize that my friends were dancing too. They were encouraging me to dance with them, but I was really hesitant. Later that day, a speaker, Paul J Kim, flipped my world upside down. He was giving his own testimony on stage and I was sucked in. I couldn't stop listening. At one point, he was talking about the Saturday Night Adoration. Somewhere in his story he said, "...and at that moment God gave me a hug." I felt a hug in that exact moment. I had no idea how to feel. I looked around as if I was going to find the person who was hugging me. I went back to my hotel room that night super confused. Fast forward to the Legendary Saturday Night Adoration. Everyone was telling me that there was going to be a really long Adoration where people laugh, cry, and rest in the Spirit among other things. Great! Wait, what?! The group I was with started getting seated and the monstrance was set on the altar with a spotlight on it. I kind of knew what a monstrance and Adoration was, but I hadn't encountered either of them. The whole time the priest was walking around, I felt really at peace. I just sat there with my eyes closed...no thoughts. My mind ever since I can remember has always been racing. I received exactly what I needed— true peace.

Cathryn Senour

"There is no fear in love, but perfect love casts out fear."

-1 John 4:18

Healthy college athletes are not supposed to wind up in the hospital with organ failure. Planes are not supposed to crash, and when they do, passengers do not usually walk away with only minor injuries. A city on a hill is not supposed to flood, and travelers should not be trapped in its flash-flooded tunnels.

All of this is not supposed to happen within a year and a half to a young woman who has not even made it to her twenty-first birthday.

Then again, kings are not supposed to sacrifice their lives for the salvation of their people. As it turns out, Jesus Himself does not follow the rules of how we think this world is supposed to work.

* * *

I grew up in a Catholic home with my parents and younger sister. We attended Mass most Sundays, I made my First Communion, and we prayed before meals and at bedtime. I dabbled in my faith after confirmation in high school by playing flute with the church choir and volunteering at retreats, and was known as the "good church girl" among my friends. I was both a rule-follower and a prankster, always getting close to the edge but never crossing the line. Those beginnings would serve me well in the later years, but like the prodigal son, I had to walk away before I could come back (Luke 15:11-32).

* * *

As a child, I was usually off in my own world, exploring the woods in our large backyard in small town, Minnesota. My parents were incredibly supportive of my younger sister and I, always encouraging us to pursue our passions. I joined the middle school track team, and quickly fell in love with hurdling (after I got over the fear of them, of course). That one choice in seventh grade launched a ten-year track and field career, and would play a huge role in my faith journey.

High school came around with a whirlwind of great friends, hard work, and accolades. Medals and plaques glistened on my bedroom walls, I had a binder full of congratulatory certificates, and my mom had an entire scrapbook dedicated to the newspaper articles written about my successes. It was a lot of pressure, and glory, placed on a teenaged-me still trying to figure out who I was and who to go to prom with. All the emphasis placed on my accomplishments diverted my attention from my identity as a daughter of God first, and rather as the track and field star who enjoyed her time in the record books.

Three months after graduating high school, I went off to college in Duluth, Minnesota. After two trips to state as a hurdler in high school, I had signed on as a sprinter on the university's track and field team. Somewhere in between studying for all the science classes I was taking to attain my hopes of physician assistant (PA) school, I fit in up to four hours a day devoted to track. I worked hard, pressing my nose to the grindstone (or a chemistry textbook).

Though God was little more than a blip on the radar my freshman year, I still attended Mass most Sundays, went to confession once a semester (though I was always incredibly nervous and dreaded the thought of confessing my sins), and would occasionally attend a Christian bible study with other athletes. My prayer life consisted of sending requests to the Big Guy when I needed him. Jesus was not my center, although I claimed He was.

In my eighteen years of life at that time, I had never had a strong Catholic friend. I didn't know what it was to have a sister in Christ who was seeking holiness. That trend continued through my first year in college. I yearned for community. My friends from high school had journeyed to different schools hours away from me. As anyone who has attended college can probably relate, I thought everyone else was having infinitely more fun than I was. My moral compass, was a strong enough beacon that I felt isolated at a public university where casual hookups and blackouts were the norm. I would go to parties think, "Is this really all there is? Where is the joy in this?". I was starved for joy and authenticity.

As the summer months shifted into the fall of my sophomore year, I threw myself into my school work and athletics. My grades were consistently near the top of the class, and I was seeing similar success on the track. On Sundays, I would sit in Mass, passively participating and occasionally drawing inspiration from the homily. Besides Mass and my infrequent prayers when I was in need of help, Jesus was still a small part of my life. I desired Him, and would have moments where I felt closeness with Him, but ultimately I had my attention elsewhere.

December brought the stress of finals and excitement of the impending winter break. I had my eyes set on relaxation and family time back home for a full month. It was not until I received a surprise phone call from a FOCUS (Fellowship of Catholic University Students) missionary that was serving on my college campus, while I was frantically studying that I considered changing my plans. At that time, I had no idea what FOCUS was, or that we even had missionaries on campus. I listened cautiously as she invited me to an upcoming FOCUS conference created for college students like myself.

Instantly, the list of excuses of why I could not make it flooded my mind. Fortunately, God in His goodness did not give up. In every single objection, God had a response.

I was very unsure of what to expect at first. Throughout the conference, I felt as if I were dipping my toes into the waters of Catholicism, not ready to fully commit my life but curious. Yet, despite my hesitancy, I encountered Christ. What a gift it is that Jesus can take just a little, "Yes," and transform our hearts.

The highlight of the conference for me was the night of Adoration. I had been to Adoration only a few times prior. At first, as I gazed upon the Eucharist in the monstrance and looked around at the other thousand college students doing the same, I felt… nothing. Nothing but this desire in my heart to go to confession.

I tried to pray more fervently. My anxiety grew worse. I just wanted to feel and see what these other students, so clearly moved by Jesus, were feeling and seeing.

Still frustrated, I knelt in prayer. "Okay, Jesus, if this is really you, I want to see it. I want to see someone tangibly moved by you." *Go to confession.* "Here I am. Change my heart." *Go to confession.*

Through the promptings of Jesus, I grudgingly made my way out of the room with Adoration. There, in the middle of the crowded hallway full of students in life for confession, was a girl about my age sobbing on the floor and crying out to God; she was moved with passion for our Lord. Others came rushing over to pray with and for her. Right in front of me was a literal answer to a prayer: someone tangibly moved by Christ.

When it was my turn for confession, I sat down facing a priest I had never met before. I took a deep breath, and began to confess. As I told the priest my offenses, I noticed this confession was far different than any other time I had been to reconciliation. In my honesty and meekness, my sins rolled off my tongue as if they were part of a poem, as if I was singing my sins to God as an offering of my love. I was washed by the blood of the Lamb and emerged clean.

The priest reminded me of the gifts God had given me, and how I must remember to thank Him. He also directed me to ask Jesus to show me when He is proud of me. At that instant, I heard (though it was not audible, it was something deeper, like a conversation straight to my heart): "*I am so proud of you right now.*" I bawled in thanksgiving, and felt as though I was floating as I made my way back to Adoration.

As I looked upon the monstrance, this time with a pure heart, I had no problem believing that piece of bread was truly Jesus. I quickly made my way up to the altar, not caring how ridiculous I must have looked shuffling around students on their knees praying. Tears rolled down my face as I knelt, knowing deep within my heart that Jesus was within feet of me, looking upon me as I gazed back at Him.

* * *

Spring semester of my sophomore year started a few weeks after the conference and brought with it new classes and the start of track season. Life sped up, and I shifted Jesus from the front to the backseat. Though I still attended Mass on Sundays and would go to Christian events on campus. I did not make time for a deep prayer life within all of my activities. A friend I had met at the conference continued to invite me to her Bible study, and with the exception of one time that I joined (and loved it!), I continued to decline her offer. My encounter with Christ changed had my heart but not my priorities.

Little did I know He would intervene in a big way in a few short months.

Making time for Christ was especially not a priority to me as I saw my race times drop. Like most of my collegiate athlete peers, I saw no issue with placing my identity in my athletic abilities. After all, I was doing great, I felt great, and I felt fulfilled. Life as a collegiate athlete had consumed me once again.

My eyes were set on competing at the national meet, and I had a pretty good chance at it. However, the month leading up to the conference meet- the last chance I had to qualify for nationals- was riddled with injuries. I would tell my coaches I was fine to race at meets, only to limp away from the finish line, unable to compete in my other events.

By the time the conference meet came, I was eager to prove myself. Despite an exceptionally miserable cough and a cold windy day, I was ready to compete. The wind whipped my hair as I anxiously walked to the starting line of the 400 meter hurdles race. I settled into the starting blocks. After an agonizing few seconds in the 'set' position, a gun crack, a step out of the blocks, I was on my way. I cleared the first hurdle and then the first 100 meters easily. Along the backstretch of the track, I ducked my head against the wind and gave everything I had, knowing my competition was slowing down against the torrent. By the 200 meter mark I had an easy lead. My coach yelled my split time, and I was on track to run my fastest 400 meter hurdles ever. I cruised around the second turn, my eyes set on the finish line. Only 100 meters left, and I would have a personal record and a time to take me to nationals.

But then.

Something instantly changed. My legs felt like lead, and each step was more difficult than the one before. I gasped for oxygen, and the world grew fuzzy. Later, spectators far in the stands would tell me that I turned a ghostly pale. With each remaining hurdle, my form crumbled further. I collapsed at the finish line with a time far from nationals-worthy.

The hour after the race was a hazy blur of teammates carrying me off the track and being evaluated by an athletic trainer. I was crushed to see the time I ran, knowing I was capable of so much more. I had wanted to please my coaches and inspire my teammates. Yet, there I was, surrounded by my coaches and teammates on the infield, vomiting and unable to stand due to dizziness and nausea.

Once our team made it back to the hotel we were staying at, I tried to stay awake with my teammates, but felt completely spent. While the rest of the girls in my room stayed up talking, I called it a night and fell asleep almost instantly.

Sometime in the middle of the night, I awoke, nauseous beyond belief. I nearly sprinted to the bathroom and vomited. I had barely made it back to my bed when I felt the same queasiness. Eventually, I succumbed to grabbing my pillow and resting on the cool bathroom tile, waiting for the next episode to strike.

Later, I awoke to deep, sharp pains on either side of my abdomen, and the familiar nausea had returned. I tried to get comfortable, but realized there was no pain-free position. With each restless turn, the pain grew worse and spread to my back.

Soon, phone alarms went off and my teammates slowly rolled out of bed and got ready. The pain in my sides grew more intense. I started to think this might be something more than just a virus. While my teammates gathered in the lobby to prepare to board our bus, I slumped along a wall. My skin was pale, I couldn't find the energy to stand, the dull ache was now a scream, and the nausea was unbearable. I caught the attention of a coach. It was time to go to the hospital.

I rode in a van with my head and assistant coach to the nearest emergency room. It was the longest few minutes of a drive I had ever experienced. We walked into the emergency department, and I was triaged right away. At that point, I figured dehydration was the source of all my troubles and I would just need to receive an IV of fluid and be on my way. An IV was started in my arm, and some blood tests were drawn. While my coaches and I waited for the results, I was led to another room for X-rays. By the time I returned, the blood results were back.

With my coaches by my side as I laid on the hospital bed, the doctor, whom I had developed a good rapport with, came into the room to discuss the results. "So, as you know, we drew a lot of different tests. On a whim, I decided to test your kidney functions. I'm glad I did," he said. "Catie, your kidneys have failed."

I sat back, looking at him with disbelief. He continued. "Given that it's the weekend and this is a small hospital, we don't have nephrologists available to treat you. We need to get you to a larger hospital, and soon." I nodded. Together, we decided I would receive my care at a large hospital near where my parents lived- and seven hours away from where I was.

We reached the large university hospital in the late evening. I cannot imagine the sight I must have been; a nineteen-year-old girl, in a hospital bed, pale-skinned too weak to walk.

In walked a resident, who introduced herself and explained to me that because it was late at night on a Saturday, the attending nephrologist (kidney specialist) was not around but would see me in the morning. I nodded, licked my popsicle, and watched the commotion around me. My IV was connected to a bag of saline, replenishing my fluids. A nurse wrote my information on a whiteboard. Blood was drawn. Pain medicine for the growing burn in my sides was given. Eventually, my room was empty except for my mom and myself.

Sleep did not come easily for me. My aching sides kept me tossing, trying to find a comfortable position. I was told I could always ask for more pain medication, and as I look back, I am unsure why I did not ask for more. The weight of the situation had not yet hit me, but I was in a strange sterile place, trying to create a home of it. Finally, I drifted off into a deep sleep.

Along with the influx of hospital staff came streams of visitors. Even on that first full day in the hospital, friends and family stopped by to bring me gifts and company. Encouraging messages flooded my phone and inbox. I felt so supported and loved through it all.

But then came nighttime. Night was the hardest. It was lonely, dark and painful. Night was the time the reality of the situation set in. Without the distraction of friends or a phone buzzing away, I was left to ponder my condition. I still was not allowed or even able to eat. All labs showed my kidneys deteriorating more with each blood draw, with no explanation. That second night, I cried myself to sleep. Tears of uncertainty. Of fear and asking why.

*   *   *

My third day in the hospital began as the one before, with a too-early needle stick. I also had a kidney biopsy, and met with my nephrologist. She began to explain the ultrasound revealed my kidneys appeared small and misshapen. The biopsy results would continue to come in over the next week. Most strikingly, however, was that the blood tests revealed my kidney function continued to decline, but also painted a very confusing picture. She let me know she had never seen anything like this, and that she would be consulting with the other nephrologists on her team.

The weight of her words washed over me, though I wanted to stay strong for my mom, whose face was filled with even more worry than before. In the rush of overwhelming information, trying to comprehend what was happening, my mom asked the doctor to repeat nearly everything she had just said. We were both overwhelmed, afraid, and unsure of what the future would hold.

* * *

That third night in the hospital was the hardest. I cried softly into my pillow, feeling the pain of my sides, the fear in my heart, the growl of a stomach that had not had solid food in over thirty-six hours. All I had known was crumbling. A collegiate athlete, in the best shape of her life, should not be in the hospital with organ failure. So, I did the one thing I knew I could do while I lost control over everything else. I prayed, like I had the past few nights in the dark quiet room of the hospital.

Jesus knows our hearts, and He knows our potential. More than anything, He loves us just the way we are. He speaks to us in a way that we will understand, crafted for our very soul. In every moment, He is reaching to us, waiting for us to reach to Him. That night in the hospital, I extended my hand back to Him, opened my heart, and spoke to Him of my fear.

In the depths of my heart, a soft whisper filled my soul. *Do you see now why your identity cannot be wrapped in things of this world?* Yes, Jesus. *The things of this world fade. The only thing remaining when all else is lost is love and relationship with others.*

Illness does something to a person's view of the world. In that moment, I saw how trivial everything else besides love was. How easily we wrap ourselves in things to keep us busy, like cellphones, approval via likes from Facebook friends, money (so much energy towards money), plans for the weekend, and all the other minute things that get in the way of the only thing that really matters: our relationship with Christ. Most importantly I saw the fault in placing my identity in my athletic abilities. How quickly that can be, and was in my case, taken away.

I drifted to sleep, the uncertainty still there, but the fear replaced by a deep peace and a confidence in healing.

* * *

The rhythm of a morning in the hospital that I had grown familiar with began once again. Blood draws, residents listening to my heart and lungs, meeting the new nurses, doctors on rounds. I was growing more comfortable in this strange environment, finding the regularity in it all and visiting with the doctors I had grown to know over the past few days. I had also become accustomed to hearing the update on my declining kidney function around mid-morning.

My morning rituals were about to change.

A confused doctor walked in with the results of my latest blood draw.

"We don't know why..." she began, "But your kidneys are getting better. The labs are all looking better. We're still trying to figure out why, but... it's good news. We also got some of the tests from your kidney biopsy, and we're just as confused about that because, well, your kidneys look perfect."

I laid in my bed, just as confused as the medical team. I had not received any sort of treatment for my kidneys, as the doctors did not know what to treat in the first place. Yet I was getting healthier.

That day, my doctors allowed me to go outside. The sun warmed my skin, and I appreciated the beauty of the world with new eyes. I sat with my dad, having a little picnic outside the emergency room doors I had entered a few nights before, and ate solid food for the first time in days.

The next day, I was discharged home.

* * *

For a few weeks after I had returned home from the hospital, I held closely to the deeper spirituality I had encountered that quiet night of accepting Jesus into my heart. Yet life quickly returned to its usual business. My kidneys became more of an annoyance than a witness of a miracle. The fatigue I had from the recovery process irritated me. Granted, my experience helped me to not grow frustrated in the small things and to appreciate the love of my family. Overall, though, I was trying to cope and move on.

Answers were hard to find. Some of the smartest nephrologists in the nation still had no idea why I went into kidney failure, why I got better, or if it would happen again. To my heartbreak, I was told I should never race my beloved 400 meter hurdles again, being that all the doctors knew was that some sort of exertion pushed me into a bad place.

As I boarded a plane to Poland for a study abroad two months following my hospital stay, I pushed back the events of my illness and instead looked forward to a European summer semester. Poland was to be an escape, a land of newness and unfamiliarity. It would also prove to be one of the most challenging tests of my faith. The nearest Catholic church, though immensely gorgeous, required a light rail trip to a street I could not pronounce (Not to mention every street name looked the exact same to me- just a jumble of consonants with a whole lot of 'k's). I made the trek one Sunday with a fellow classmate, but the other weeks no one was interested in going, and I was afraid to go alone. I would read the readings for Sundays alone and take a moment for reflection, and marvel at the cathedrals we would tour in Krakow, Wroclaw, and Prague, but still, I went over a month without the Mass. Sundays were spent adventuring through cities, not Church.

By the time I returned to America, I hungered for the Eucharist in a way I had never experienced. I felt empty. Without. Lacking the strength to pursue my faith. The gift of Christ, hidden in the Eucharist, is the greatest mystery and also our greatest nourishment. Nonetheless, even with my desire for the Mass, I just wanted to meld back into the life I had been living, one where Jesus was there when I needed Him, but not the center of my life. Like the prodigal son, I had confidence in my inheritance, but was squandering it away.

Thank you, thank you, thank you Jesus for knowing my heart so well, for never abandoning me, and for shaking my world again after that summer semester.

* * *

It was a sunny, beautiful August day a few weeks after my return from Poland and a few days before I was headed back to college when my whole world would flip upside down- quite literally.

My dad, sister, and I stood on a sandy beach listening to a pilot's instructions, excited to board a sea plane in northern Minnesota to see the beautiful forests surrounding Lake Superior from a bird's-eye view. I originally wanted to stay back with my mom, but my persuasive extroverted 'fear of missing out' had me with my dad and sister; headset on and eager to fly.

We strapped in, the pilot and my sister in the front and my dad and myself seated in the back. The engine roared; we accelerated across the top of the lake, the pilot slowly raised the plane off the water, and then we were airborne. Trees became tiny dots across a green landscape and lakes became small blue puddles. As I looked out below, I was afraid of the height we had reached, but also in awe of the view.

The plane needed to be refueled, so we stopped at a small station along the side of a lack in the middle of the wilderness. We made small talk with the men who helped us. "We always watch every plane that takes off from here until we can't see it so we know it's safe," The men told us.

After filling up, we buckled in and the plane rumbled back to life. Our pilot started guiding the plane across the lake, gaining speed. Within seconds, we were up in the air again, the lake becoming smaller outside the window. As we were about to clear the towering pine trees on the other side of the lake from where we began, I felt the plane drop almost instantly in altitude. "Hold on," the pilot tersely said. I heard the fear in his voice as he frantically wrestled with the plane's controls. The plane rocked, but we continued upward.

Within a few seconds, everything turned for the worse. The engine roared, but gravity pulled back harder. We quickly lost altitude, jostling as the plane brushed along tops of pine trees. A small swamp emerged. I stared at the water straight below me, feeling the speed at which we were nearing the swamp. We were traveling much too fast to result in any semblance of a controlled landing, not to mention we were nearly vertical.

The thing about crisis situations is that you do not get to control what you think. Our bodies go into fight-or-flight mode. I went into "fight" mode, evaluating my scenario and what actions need to happen next to preserve my life. I wish, in those last few seconds before I knew we had crashed, that I had prayed for the protection of my family or for the forgiveness of my sins. Instead, as I looked down at the water, I thought, "Of course this would happen."

I had been spurned by having kidney failure. Subconsciously, my brain had codified that event into my mind as a signal that horrible, rare events were to be my norm. There was no surprise in my mind that we were crashing. My second thought: I hoped I wouldn't be paralyzed. Because then I could not run in track. I think it is important to mention these few details because it shows right were my priorities were. Though I had in theory chosen to make Jesus a priority, I still saw myself first and foremost as an athlete and I was not willing to abandon that or place anything else, even pursuing sainthood, in front of that.

We hit. We hit hard. First on one of the plane floats, and then the other. We then launched off the water, flipping in the air. My head whacked against the window with a loud crack. The plane landed upside-down. Water rushed in. The pilot tried to push against the doors. They would not open. The wings had pushed up against the doors, blocking our exit. The thought of drowning crossed my mind. I did not want to die that way.

The water stopped filling up right above our heads.

We had crashed just shallow enough, and miraculously, everyone was fine.

Acting quickly, the pilot shut off all of the mechanical equipment, including the radio, to prevent a fire in the event gasoline had leaked. He unbuckled my sister, who splashed in the water below her. With force, he managed to open the window that I had hit my head on. I slid out sideways and feet first onto the plane wing and then stepped into a muddy swamp. My sister followed. The window was too small for my six-foot-tall dad. He slammed into the door on the opposite side and safely exited the plane as well.

Muddy water covered my legs up to my knees as the four of us stood on the shore. We were surrounded by forest with no way to communicate. None of us had a cell phone, though we did have a camera, and took a few pictures of the scene. Without much lead on a direction to go, we walked into the quiet Minnesota woods.

Within a couple hundred yards, the forest cleared into a perfectly manicured lawn. A man walked towards us, and I cannot imagine what his first thought must have been seeing four strangers standing on his remote property, covered in mud, blood, and bruises. "Hi..." The pilot started. "Do you have a phone? We just crashed in the swamp over there," He gestured. We could hear car horns off in the distance from people who must have seen the crash, looking for survivors.

An hour later, I laid in a hospital bed, again in a small town emergency room that summer. It was there, waiting for the results of my CT scan (which would show only a minor concussion), that Jesus spoke to me, so clearly, so directly to my heart, that I could not miss it.

I need you to be a leader in your faith.
"What? I don't know if you've noticed, Jesus, but I haven't been living a life worthy of being a leader."
Silence.
He meant His word.

This all occurred on the feast of Saint Monica, a woman who became a saint after relentlessly praying for her child, Saint Augustine, a prodigal son in his own right, to return to the Church.

*   *   *

The Federal Aviation Administration would rule the crash "pilot error"' after having no other explanation. This was a skilled pilot, though, someone who flew for a tourist business. The crash was a string of miracles. We had lost altitude just far enough out that we did not free-fall into the pine trees, which would have likely resulted in a fire. The swamp provided a clear enough landing field, and the water was just shallow enough that we did not sink with the doors blocked. No fuel had leaked from the airplane. All passengers walked away. However, it would take me a while to see the crash as a miracle, and not a curse.

Just a few days after the crash, school started up and I was back in classes. Deep purple bruises littered my legs, and a gash ran across my forehead. School work took twice as long with the breaks I needed from looking at the computer screen. At first I was able to speak of the crash as if it did not affect me, as if I were telling the story of someone else. Slowly, as the weeks went on and everyone moved on with their lives, I was struggling to keep up. Fear and anger welled within my heart. The questions that at first had been a whisper began to yell out. Why me? What if I make another choice that will land me in the hospital? Why can't I have answers?

I grew distant from God, my growing frustration and mistrust stacking more bricks onto my wall separating myself from Jesus. The question of, "If God can save me from a plane crash, why would he even let it happen in the first place?" festered in my heart. I no longer trusted He had my best interest in mind. In my heart, I believed the closer I grew to Him, the more bad things would happen to me. I did not think of Him as a loving father. I saw Him as absent, ignorant and uncaring of my pain (Which could not be further from the truth).

A month after returning to school, I found myself on a retreat with the university's Catholic group. Honestly, I am not sure what compelled me to go. It was a retreat intended for those who had never gone on a retreat, and primarily freshman. I fit into neither category, so I can only attribute my presence there to someone praying for me.

There was an opportunity for confession one of the nights. I knew I needed to go, but I was deeply torn in two ways. First, I had become so angry at God, though I knew deep within my heart I was wrong. Second, I had failed so many times to living up to a Christian standard, even after (as I viewed it) God had given me two chances to see the fragility of life and the importance of turning to Him. Like the prodigal son who saw his complete failings and thought he should be treated only as a hired worker and not as a son by his father, I saw my complete unworthiness of God's mercy and grace.

Despite all of this, as I faced the priest, I knew I was looking at the face of Christ in His mercy. I spoke of my anger at God, the lack of trust I had held onto, the fear of daily life and the what-ifs. The priest looked upon me with such gentleness and understanding, and said something along the lines of, "It's okay to tell God these things. Let Him hear your anger. Let Him know your fear. What is better - to refuse to talk to someone when you're mad, or to open conversation, even if you are in the wrong?" Tears filled my eyes. All this time, I felt this anger, but never told Jesus, because I had been told to never be angry with God. Yet, there I was, angry with God, even though I knew He was only good.

Following the retreat, in my room alone, cuddled up on a chair, I unleashed all of my emotions to God. I started silently, but soon enough I was talking, crying, uninhibited.

"Why would you do this to me? How can I believe you love me? Why can't I live a normal life? Why do I live in fear?"

Answers did not come instantly, because God in His grace knew I was embarking on a journey, not arriving at a destination. Instead, what I received in that moment was more in what I gave, extending my hand back to God. Just like the father greeted his son from a long way off, Jesus came to me. He met me where I was at; He did not demand I become far more holy and perfect before He would love me. Jesus was only awaiting my invitation to walk with me.

I often think of what that walk home between the prodigal son and his father would have been like. The son must have felt so ashamed, so unworthy, that he walked slowly, reacquainting himself with his father. Meanwhile, the father would have been so patient, so loving, not hurrying the pace, just happy to have his son back in his presence. Over and over again, the father must have repeated how much he loved the son, in that moment, no matter where he had been or how he had hurt the father.

Following the retreat, my junior year was like that slow walk with the father. I was still timid, but the more familiar I grew with my Father and the more I understood His love, the more eager I was to trust in Him. Once, in confession, a priest wisely gave me a penance of allowing God to love me back. As I prayed, it was then that I realized I had been yearning for Jesus' acceptance, but He had loved me all along. I did not understand how completely Jesus loved me, how much He loved all of us, even though I had hurt him so frequently. He was still walking beside me; there was nothing I could do to cause Him to turn and walk away from me.

I started going to Bible study weekly and praying more frequently, and desired to be a witness of God's love to my teammates and friends. In all of this, though, I felt very lonely and isolated. My core group of friends was not comprised of people searching after a relationship with Jesus. I prayed and begged for good, Catholic friends, waiting on the Lord to send them. Still, I persevered, chasing after Jesus, even if at times my "chase" was more of a crawl.

During this time, I also ignored all of the doctors' advice, and continued racing on the track team. I was able to compete, but was slower than before. Nationals was no longer on my radar, and looking back now, I am grateful for that. God allowed me to continue doing what I love but without the speed I once had; it no longer consumed my life or my identity. Instead, I began praying with teammates before races, and would picture Jesus at the finish line of the 100 meter hurdles (I very rarely ran the 400 meter hurdles following my illness, though I occasionally would at the request of my coach), with His arms wide open waiting for me. I hoped arriving at heaven would be just like that.

* * *

Junior year ended, and I was eager to enjoy my first summer in my college town. Through the previous year, I had grown closer to Jesus. However, there was a part of me still so fearful of giving myself entirely to Christ. If I were to live only for Jesus, what would I become? Who would I spend my time with? Would people think I was too weird- a 'Jesus freak,' and give up on trying to understand my new life? What would I do on the weekends? At 20 years old, stuck in between two different lives, the choice was not coming easily even though I knew what was right. Instead of making a choice on purpose, I slid into comfort.

On June 17th of that year, I wrote in my journal that I was slipping, having trouble accepting the teachings of Catholicism, and that I knew I was not spending enough time with Christ. On June 20th, my journal had a new entry, detailing a life changed and brought back to Jesus once again.

After a long shift as a nursing assistant, I was eager to climb into bed. Rain pelted my car roof as I turned the key. It was nearly midnight and the roads were quiet. My small car sprayed water from puddles as I started my drive home. It had rained all day in a kind of barrage I had never seen before. Forecasters were shocked with the storm's magnitude, longevity, and intensity. As I made my way home, storm sewers were at the maximum capacity, and my headlights illuminated the water pouring back onto the street. I cautiously steered my car around the pooling water, knowing my tiny vehicle was no match for anything more than a puddle.

I merged onto the freeway and neared the first of three tunnels I needed to pass through before my exit. A police car that had been driving next to me stopped on the highway and reversed. Though I was confused, I figured he was on a call. However, as I entered the tunnel, I saw he did not reverse to go some*where*, but rather to avoid some*thing*: a flooded tunnel.

Within seconds, my car was surrounded by water, growing deeper every second. I felt trapped. In a few short moments, I weighed my options. I could either continue to drive with the possibility that my car would get swept away and I would lose control, or, I could get out of my car and try to walk through the long tunnel, risking my life as the water rose, not knowing how deep it would become. If I made it out of the tunnel, I would have to walk out on the flooded freeway until help could come. Ultimately, I chose to drive, staying close behind a minivan directly ahead of me. A pickup truck ahead of the minivan had a snow plow attached to the front, even though it was June, and parted the waters as it drove.

Fear swept over me. I wanted to call my parents, but they were on vacation in Europe and I was unable to reach them. I decided to call my best friend. She answered to my frantic voice. "I'm trapped. I'm not sure I'm going to make it."

I heard her say, "What?", right as I lost cell phone service in the tunnel.

In the darkness, I clung to God, praying for protection. Instantly, in my worried heart I heard, *"When you pass through waters, I will be with you; through rivers, you shall not drown."* Over and over, the verse repeated in my soul. Eventually, I made it out of the first tunnel. Then the second. Then the last. I exited the freeway, and drove up the steep hill to my home. Man-hole covers were floating above their openings, water gushing out onto the streets. With each stoplight, I thanked Jesus for my safety.

Eventually, I arrived at my house, collapsed on my bed, and cried. I was like a toddler who was finally done throwing a tantrum. I was done fighting with God, and was ready to be His. Finally, I trusted in His protection. Though I still wrestled with the meaning of suffering, I trusted that His ways were greater than mine. After all, He had agonized on the cross, and understood the experience of human suffering. He gently spoke, so clearly yet again, "*I want your whole heart.*" This time, I said yes. And I meant it.

After all, all Jesus truly desires is for us to love Him with the same intensity He loves us. Though we fail time and time again, He stays beside us because His love never ends. I committed myself that night to continue to walk alongside the Father; that even when I would get distracted, I would turn my eyes back to Him. He could have all of me.

I knew in that moment the flood would have great significance for the rest of my life, and in my journal the next morning I wrote, "Lord, in that moment You showed me You would be my protector. I want to give You my all. I want to never falter. I hope You will always and forever hold onto me and pull me back to last night." I knew I needed to remember the moment I gave Him my heart, and why.

Later, I found out the tunnels were closed right after I had driven through. The rain had flooded the rivers that ran from the top of the hill to Lake Superior, and a dam had failed. Residents awoke to feet of water in their streets and homes. Entire roads were washed away. Lake Superior, usually pristine and clear blue, was now a murky, muddy brown. College students kayaked around town to visit their friends and residents tried out their jet skis on the mall-parking-lot-turned-lake. Within a few days, I was following FEMA trucks on my way to do errands.

What strikes me most, though, is the verse God had placed in my heart that night. It was from Isaiah 43:2. The chapter title: Promises of Redemption and Restoration. He helped me to return to Him. He redeemed and restored my soul.

* * *

Senior year started, and I was committed to serving Christ. I was invited to be a student missionary with FOCUS. I led a bible study with my track and field team. I was so grateful to have a new role on the team that year: captain. It was a testament that God does not always choose the fastest or the strongest to lead; He just needs a willing and loving heart. Though I continued to struggle with sin, as we all do, this time I was committed to turning right back to Christ. As I continued my pre-medicine classes, I surprised myself when I accepted an offer to be a FOCUS missionary following graduation from undergrad instead of going straight on to PA school as was my plan.

Jesus has continued to bless me with a beautiful, sometimes unpredictable life. I served two wonderful years with FOCUS, meeting college students right where they were and introducing them to the person of Jesus Christ. My faith deepened through witnessing their growth - it is truly in giving we receive! It was an arduous journey when I felt the call to leave FOCUS (a testimony in and of itself), but I was so thankful for both the call to FOCUS and for the call to move to the next chapter of life. I took a leap of faith and moved to Colorado for PA school, where I have now lived for nearly four years. I am now working in my dream job as a PA in pediatric medicine. I still feel like a missionary, a witness to Christ's love within my field, though it looks a little different now (and with fewer late-night pizza parties compared to my FOCUS days). I also recently embarked on a new adventure a year ago- marriage to a fantastic, Godly man who I met within my first year living in Colorado. I am so joy-filled at this opportunity to grow closer to Christ through this new call and vocation.

* * *

Whenever I share the testimony God gave to my life, I always add a caveat. God speaks to each one of us in a way unique to our heart. In His goodness, He knew my stubborn little heart needed more of a yell than a whisper. Yes, I have had some major events in my life that led me to Christ, but it is not the events that are important. It is the turning of the heart back to Jesus, who never stops pursuing each of us. This story would be nothing if I had refused to return to God in each opportunity. I firmly believe tales of continuous days in prayer with a slowly growing and changing heart can be just as powerful and transformative testimonies as the dramatic tales. The journey God has given you is beautiful because it is His.

Jesus and I are still on the walk home together. Knowing how graciously the father in the tale of the prodigal son welcomed his child home, I am so eager to encounter the Lord in His fullness in heaven.

Praise be Jesus Christ, now and forever.
Mother Mary, keep us, guard us, and protect us
under your mantle. Amen.

Epilogue

I just want to say thank you so much for taking the time to read our testimonies! It can be hard to be vulnerable and share such intimate encounters we have with our Lord, but it can also be so inspiring and uplifting to hear how God is working in people's lives. So don't allow these stories to just be stories. God is working in your life too, so don't be afraid to share your testimony of His mercy!

Tricia Walz